AF477945

ABSENCE
IS SUCH A
TRANSPARENT
HOUSE

ABSENCE
IS SUCH A
TRANSPARENT
HOUSE

poems by

ABY KAUPANG

TEBOT BACH • HUNTINGTON BEACH • CALIFORNIA • 2011

© 2011 Aby Kaupang. All rights reserved. No part of this book may be used or reproduced in any manner whatsoever without written permission except in the case of brief quotations embodied in critical articles and reviews.

For information, address Tebot Bach Permissions Department, Box 7887, Huntington Beach, CA 92615-7887 USA.

Design, layout, cover design: Tania Baban-Natal, Conflux Press
Cover art and drawings: Jaime Gustavson. (http://jaimegustavson.com)
Author photo: Christine Peak

ISBN 13: 978-1-893670-69-3
ISBN 10: 1-893670-69-4

Library of Congress Control Number: 2011925196

A TEBOT BACH BOOK

Tebot Bach, Welsh for little teapot, is A Nonprofit Public Benefit Corporation which sponsors workshops, forums, lectures, and publications. Tebot Bach books are distributed by Small Press Distribution, Armadillo and Ingram.

THE TEBOT BACH MISSION

Tebot Bach is dedicated to strengthening community, promoting literacy and broadening the audience for poetry by demonstrating through readings, workshops, and publications, the power of poetry to transform human experience.

This book is made possible by a grant from The San Diego Foundation Steven R. and Lera B. Smith Fund at the recommendation of Lera Smith.

www.tebotbach.org

{ *ave atque vale* }

for Sue Van Schoonhoven & John Biasiolli

| ACKNOWLEDGMENTS

{The author is grateful to the following}

for their illuminations, longitude of clemency, & consideration of communes, motor scooters, guitars & of course, sometimes, poetry: Sasha Steensen, Gordon Hadfield, Kristy & Dan Beachy-Quick, Stephanie & Arnie G'Schwind, Bill Tremblay, Mary Crow, Kevin Ward, Marty Moran, Logan Burns, Micah Cavaleri, Chloe Leisure, Kevin Foskin, Rebecca Wolff, D.A. Powell, Craig Morgan Teicher, Janet Holmes, and Elizabeth Robinson., & Clyde Lehmann.

for those who birthed this: editress deluxe, Mifanwy Kaiser, contest judge, Gail Wronsky, and artist | friend, Jaime Gustavson

for editors and readers of the following journals in which poems from *Absence* initially appeared: *Basalt, Caketrain, delirious hem, H_NGM_N, La Petite Zine, Little Red Leaves, Lo-ball, Matter, PANK, Parcel, VOLT,* and *Word for/Word.*

and quite perhaps most intensely for her deepest loves and greatest absolvers who kept with her while she lived this manuscript: All those Kaupangs and Coopermans but especially Momma, Matthew, Elias and the illusory Maya.

Little "g" gods and almond trees and "the dead/perfume of flies," and "copses" becoming "corpses" and a most richly detailed and populated "Nothingness," and I don't want to think "Emily Dickinson" but I seem to keep thinking of her as I read this book of oddly both voluptuous and spartan poems written with an almost otherworldly amount of self-possession, of certainty in craft. This poet's concerns are Dickinson's concerns: death, what eternity is, the effusions and miracles of the natural world, the dependencies and fortitudes of the self, and yet the rhythms and diction here are entirely unique, as these stanzas from the poem "we go to the garden of swords and fire   and go" demonstrate:

> . . . a turn of a wheel a slight of eye and the whole
> spinning doe of a whirl flips into a ravine
> is it any wonder
> this blip isn't less livid
>
> even the underworld articulates emergency
> and snarling and poppies startling
> in their sudden orangeness
>
> these are sights I could leave for
> accidentally—my driving eye drawn
> to a plosive upward band of poppy
>
> and trash and glamorously
> smashing vessels nested
> in car in body in cell in souly bits of bloom . . .

Theology is one of the threads Aby Kaupang sews into these poems—a theology without piety or pedantry ("there's a trinity of endlessness/life   death   or both/which is what you are," she writes in the poem "winter sews its ice grey thread about everything." And there is both a delight in and a skepticism about language ("maroon bells, anise hyssop, compact innocence/it's the tags not the roots that are shoddy," from the poem "I swear to you the beds here were born with teeth,") I find altogether refreshing and rare.

You'll notice that the poet has named the four sections of her book "Symphyses" (Symphysis I, II, III, and IV). It's a bold gesture, as the word is so unfamiliar, so specific to medical discourse, and yet the payoff is enormous. Doing so, Kaupang could be said to be inventing a poetic form—one rich with resonance and possibility—out of this term for the articulation of bone, for the way bones grow and heal, evoking as she does the visual similarities between bones and lines (both sometimes out of necessity broken) and at the same time wisely suggesting that bone itself is articulate, that poetry, like marrow, resides deeply and actively there. I'm sure Emily Dickinson would have agreed that it does.

All in all, *Absence is such a Transparent House* is a breathtakingly original debut book of incredible certainty, poise, intelligence, energy, and depth. I feel quite honored to introduce it to you.

—*Gail Wronsky*

| *prelude* |

a woman chooses a bird and buries it

beneath her tongue
of course

     beneath the bud

a plume

when you roll away her lips

when you breathe your spirit
through her hands

when her funerary blanket withers
in your palm

          a synonym

millions of cockatiels ignite on a landing

a Mackie Daphne

                    lucents in June

I am pinned to your lantern

amid the battery of elms and fervor

{rustle}

yards echo violently

what sudden lightening in a torso
what Rorschach of angst song

what cellular weeping reading weeding laddered foothold

derived you

        first

what can I write to help you char your own spell?

symphysis one |

some momentary awareness

if I believe in other worlds   the dead

are not in this   earthly, this empty
tied to this earth   this canopy
push-pin earth   other-worldly   the pain

I thought   entering this   that I might
evaporate   like The Loved evaporates
and leaves this earth in palliation

Death's voice   when Death came
was a filibuster of the fomenting screech
locking the courts of my earth

if I believe in other worlds
then I have want for trespass   other worlds
not my earth now   but the Loved's

limb beside limb   enter the falter-

line of ague & darkness

similar indoors/out   the luminosity
leaves in increments   & edges

it is still the same   stagnant
still at hand   still groping here & there-ish

all the coming & going of life
and –lessness:

it's just a getting-thru:
my palliations & my symphyses

the bloom of my mouth

                            is an alter-

ing thrive   an unseasonable watery
casket of flowers   is a tender
of the brightliest
thing   shadowed in scent

blue eye   in the rafters
heaven   is reticent
bloom tisket   floor flower
book cutter   ring singing

                         the morning
folded in hedges   collapsed into cranes

and viewed the room speculatively

death being a code   the possibly oncoming

is delicious
          if it's not an ambush
of gadgets   then it's something like it

latent in apparent
tranquility and *oh blessed assurance*

this anxiety's abysmal   my lack
of lack

and then a landmine

the hand gropes everywhere
with no front line
                    to be confronted

I remembered where I was wept

not having found a name   I lacked
candles   measured alarm   and sowed
poppies in my pockets for the furrows

in my confinement   I said "god

hem me in"   what can I do
with my mono-eyed loving

bullet unbearable   enormous
& frail at night   these candelas

of attention
are heaving—

we go to the garden of swords and fire   and go

and post our signs of melting about it   we are timid
in our thawing spot   faltering if we stop there

there   the inconceivable surprise   living
living with It   the shock   our hand falls

a turn of a wheel a slight of an eye and the whole
spinning doe of a whirl flips into a ravine—

is it any wonder
this blip isn't less livid

even the underworld articulates emergency
and snarling and poppies startling
in their sudden orangeness

these are sights I could leave for
accidentally—my driving eye drawn
to a plosive bank of poppy

trash and glamorously
smashing vessels nested
in car in body in cell in souly bits of bloom

{ I look for Sue

stem and sudden Sue
not seep or splay but crack
neck }

what closes in on me   concerns me alone

this is my deaths I'm anxious for
but there you are

you too   living

with a life unable—unable to parry
unable to flee   unable to retreat—peering
through the window {both wall & sacred

absence}   waiting for illumination
or at slightest   defense

from the bone carrier offing in your alley

to scatter stones and gather them

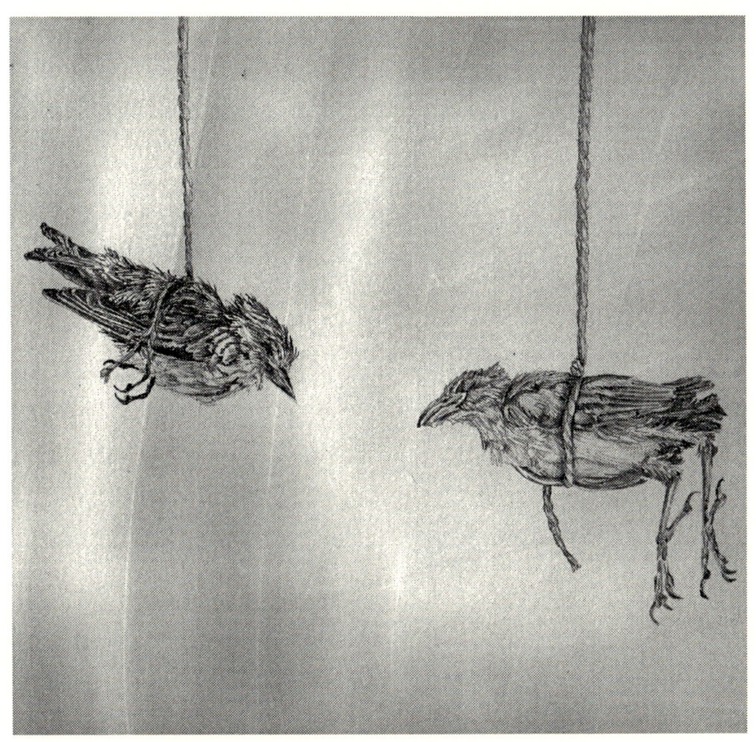

{admittance}

I am a girl with a flawed pelt

my mouth   hinges
on interpretation

tongue speech builds the self
tongue ink silences
men   but my god
arrives

with revelations incantation
and elucidation

for the utterance
of mystery
          is a case of design

tongue under roof
wandering

we are foreigners   girls
under a steeple
tongues signing for the incredulous

I am the one tonguing in flesh
the acolyte with torn light hair

                 gift me   god

Someone to interpret
          {*cori cori cori cori kana nai*}

some Name to translate

{tongues}

kiririri me ca la dost tiruana
se duria fe me kani kani kani
o sepularania do la fey kiri
manini ta nana los cori

cori cori cori cori kana nai

se duria fe me o sepularania
maninini kiririri don taria fe
sworni sworni sepularania

{paralysis}

for every mouth an answer   mimesis
for the falling downs   tongues and self
are a steeple   rising   the tongue
is a case of architecture
                              roofs blow up

come then   invitations
lofty like cantors and vulgarity

when or if   precision
is unattainable is anonymity
I worship
                    my god

my god is a god is an utterance of mystery
a word gone out numerously   swelling

are not my poems
an attempt
to translate
my god
is a cymbal drawn out

my god
              I tire

I mean to say are You not the name and the naming
of time now lived at the end of the day a new
name and the name in truths   precise?

{communion}

the manna's often stale
borrowed   in a gross way
the acolytes lie

over   the altar   make love
to little "g" god   their gusty
breaths   sweat-wrapped gifts

& screams (faking it & pleasured)
are like my screams (faking it
& pleasured) screams

on this side   I alter
                              so resemblance:

I have asked for god's remembrance
of me   little "g" says *do this*

                    {*do me*}

{Soak}

Little "g" god grows tired of me
& this my drowning day.

>They say I seem wrung.
>What a drench
>of tongue I am.

me, a tender haunting in the glass beneath the waves
me, a blessed peacemaker
me, tonguing Chiron for his skiff
me, my own My Heavy—

>tentacle on lip.

{Ecclesia}

my dove in the cleft of the rock

my hiding place   my city
the beginning of my face, your face
is the beginning
of recall   & grace

              is a grove

of almond trees   blooming   is books
there are many & their endings like bodies
are wearisome
                  you say better a day of naissance
            than the insatiable stimming of eyes

when I applied my madness
of erasure
              {windthrows   woman throws}
no one was long remembered

                              I am a fool
or wise   & this too is semantics

god lays such burden on us—eternity

in our hearts   inconceivable our skins
to fathom the doings & daily

here is reverence: belief in all things
possibled & dying

better are mouthfuls
of tranquility than wingfuls
of toil & wind & cords
                    restlessly snapping

this all comes without meaning
the way you depart in darkness
& in darkness   your name
is shrouded

                    better what the eye
sees when the almond tree blooms
when the skin drags itself
along & desire is no longer stirred

{living tombs}

1.

the body   {the body outside
the baby}   the skin with a button "lock"
refuses to eat   swerves inward
by the slight
            of exhibition

this is the baby   stasis
soundless the baby
an abhorrence of lips   waits
at the carousel   waits

the body   {the body mumbled
lock}   abdomen falcate   refuses to eat
startles at the motion divide

2.

integration is action   unperceivable
for the corpse   at the site   waits
a carousel   waits   near the cathedral   empties

a warren of bodies {the carousel} eats
mouths at the waiting
            the rain {plummets} {pluits} the babies

the ones with locks   mouth
all the cathedral won't button

3.

the lock on the skin empties
a hallway   the hallway ephemeral   leads

nowhere   daily   an architect
removing the passage   removes
the pluits   the evacuees   the exhibits

such integrate
the stoma   the falcate coma

what a warren of babies {the body}
of static locks   swerving inwards at the slight
of sidewalks and invitations
of carousal

4.

                the carousel   refusing to eat
runs static   soundless   hauls the abhorrent
lips   into a copse

that corpse   {that one in the chamber}
integrates   acts imperceptibly   bows
the falcate rain

soundless
startled

the baby {that renaissance of carousel}

swerves inward
mouths at a pluit of locks

{Ecclesia cont...}

my dove is a cleft of rocks   hiding

in cities in places beginning
with faces begging for cognizance
& grace
                groves of almond trees

bloom & books bloom   & there
there are many endings of bodies
{wearisome bodies}

                        beating a day of dying
I'm stimming
                death is insatiable

like an eye half-applied
for madness   half for erasure
& wind throws   & we throw & no

syntax is long remembered

such a burden on eternity   living with god

in our hearts   our unconcealed skins
feature the daily doings

it's possible reverence   is nothing
but a belief in dying
               in all things a toll

a dovetail of toil   a fistful of wind
the cords of tranquility sparring

a way without meaning departs in darkness
dark shrouded   a name for dark eyes   betters

the almond eye blossoms & trees drag
their desires to the sad bins of rot

{resurrection}

cast your bread upon water

cast your returns
upon the weary
the dead
perfume of flies

is an error spelling her dark names
in dark books & light books

& relenting
          her cavernous rest

a place another has vacated

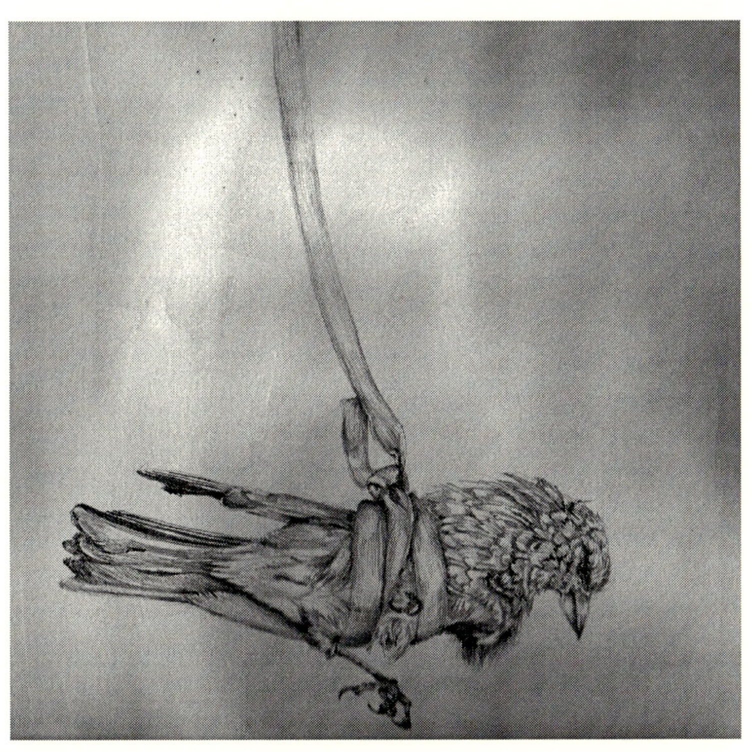

there was a funeral

a father   an ancient
low tree   a hillside   a green valley
startlings of mint fields
sprigs near the flourish
of cherries —
                    a dullness of idyll

her rings were a transom
her guitar was a transom   her name and lack—

her smash in transom   a transom

I hardly remember the days

after she died—many people
say this about grieving—it's a burrowing

a boundary   an untouchable isolation   it fumbles
as a soulish generosity *gives gives gives*
from doorways to profuse love to unoccupied rooms

grieving is a smudge I lay in
grieving the fierce train railing

what is death to me now

now it is for those in the room
a hallowed production—like birth
but backwards   a vacuous thievery of the loved

there is much grief in both

I worry that I romanticize
but tremulous
tremendous the presentness   today even

I'm rimmed
I'm stimming

I'm stimming

the wraithlike invitation into Nothingness

creeps in on me   fingers
slow fingering me

someone exactly placed it
on my bruised palm's doormat

I called it rhapsodic
improvisational

      since then
      I'm anxious always

always the fatigue   that snatch of rapture
the one I   as part of all fleshes
suffer   it's accompanied

I accompany it everywhere

two voices call me
nescio…..et excrucior

so in my smallness & accusatives

god I am small
a small small
a waiting to child again   small

if I do inhabit innumerable spaces
I inhabit them   with paucity
like bright skin   like distant spheres
I inhabit like lifting

—the difficulty of encircling anything
thought & full & kindness of sadness
& miasmic & small small night beasts

I rent them

my so thick   it's unrentable   this veil
this is all renting   every role
red

it locks on me   locks me lonely

I know this   the husband knows this   all husbandry
knows Isolation is not quiet

                  it's a banshee call
played out: as much as life
is love   love is lossly

it claims a me that barely lives

my space conforms to the vacuum
what heat | I'm unable

oblivions   anxiety   their voids gape upward

I can't shape a form of my own

in the hope of wholeness   death enters

I could speed this up
do less   perch in darkness
more permissively   be entered
                              interred

I am suggesting borderlessness
is an accumulation of yellow
& green & grey   puddling

I could ask to clip the golden dove's tail
I could just turn myself away

one takes one's place   in a pose

another has vacated   one is
birthed   by lending forms
to the forces of one's birth

one's birth is form   filled in & died in

every beginning then requires a smudging
a giving off of the pelt   near the seem
a new glass   for the squinting of the eye

Nothingness   wrapped us in cord   new skins & gave
a place for ritual   a body crossable   a border crossed

{we are afraid too   of finding
astonishment unsurpassable
like joy—total and totally new}

sometimes   force and sense swell up

in excess   the skin fields itself
constraining the territory or making amends

for chance

in love—

we fall   in love   with vacated forms
{these peoples   others   might also love}
 replaceable: we|them|or

or

all one's energies would improvise skills
one would touch at the confines of death

one would dine with it:

the venture   the hitch glitch   that love
one would die with it

what light

what light
what not light   Dark
in the alley   {motion}
where Nothingness is not yet

come home

some bodies are coffins and we sense it

some   snowing at the limits   flinch
to tighter chambers   simple cots
far from the limits of melt

but the void that opens up
isolates a me   I feels
myself trembling with anxiety

{someone's phosphorescence dims|
someone's anxious | someone's prophesying graves}

anxiety
is a form   the form I took
on dying   —not my force

in which Nothingness
posited its being
in my earthen locker

in which Nothingness
found being {tensions all hewn in}
in a inked realm

in which Nothingness
in an icy fetal lockbox
corded my contractions

sparrows in the cold die

bees die in the sun
burrowing furs in the dim earth die
stars die in the void of universes

tragedy too might die
silent rim

silent eye—

what one eats is destroyed and no

longer real — a grievous error
on earth but in heaven   one
consumes & is consumed by god
{muscularly   not our}

                        god & god's
will to seize us

$$\frac{\text{death}}{\text{nothingness}} = \frac{\text{determination}}{\text{life}}$$

{Heidegger}

{three angels canting}

1.   we wait for god and god's will waits to seize us

2.   god   my brute necessity
          is perfectly
                              nonpresent

3.   if

        god wants me   god will

        find me

in the hedges of loving kindness

there are delineations I misunderstand
mansions and Thee and ice

anything that has shape is cheating
life and death are endless

        what I fear most is evident in the saying

it is always contradictory
our houses have transparent walls
the dogwood blossoms brown in their golden borders

I can't make a new room for us

shapes make the living too cramped
the darkness of my evening house
is far more formal than the shutters themselves

how do I remember margins   threads
lines or what frays—

                how do I stop it
                how do I eat it

or how am I abandoned needing and alive
groping for the room weightless in gold lights
not knowing where I would leave to
if not beyond shutters

                my friend
                animate yet not alive
                or dead yet so fully present

what other under this

what of her   where   which groove or cove

or cliff of pines or past which cumulous
doorframe is she   which obsidian cave
of Lethe-ly wonder holds her new attentions

& not her   not her is that heaven coffin
doing what scars and broken
bodies do—sliding skins & hair when windless
stills to unreal real-er

so unrepresentative of life   what happens in the preservation

winter sews its azurine thread about us

choking and hemming

there's a trinity of endlessness
life   death   or both
which is what you are

my friend nothing or all three or
when I write thou

I must not say *you* but *yellow light*
of me

          or I and thou is Thou

and not now is endlessness

likewise my loved one—

I will never see her again

widen eye widen eye strain & nothing
she kept coming through

I couldn't see it   but they
those that loved around me

did—they found me
asleep in her jade scarf

nothing else   no one else
pulsing others out

attention—the rarest & purest

my Thou is the bloom of my mouth|my rib is afloat in fen

I blooming ever more gravely
blooms before you

so the furrow of origin
turns under   plumes

a bride when the bluffs are plucked
is pulled from the rib of man's side

|

I am that bird
I'm drawn from your rib
your side is a flung-wide ridge

|

where is origin? where heat
or blade or ruse of exaggeration?

|

my Thou is the dithering of ridges flung open
my Thou is a stasis of incomprehensible approach
my Thou is for whom the talus ascends

dusking sheets loom over a pastel cliff
cactus   columbine   scree   in a flourish
one could almost loose a life

my Thou is a tender uproot

|

when the buttes are lifting up
and the field of origins slips under

come Thou

|

come Bride

or {come} bird waters
or just flay it out

|

my rib is afloat in fen

|

my Thou you're the bloom of my mouth

was broken
{glasses, windshield, dharma}
memento a|mori & the unseemliness
of sky & mouth & now
sheets—

a normal
in loving her {manuscripts, rose bushes}
a fury   a lens   a synesthesia

or urge to crash
disconnects and reconnects
a symphysis of now
it's thubby in thouse
with the mouth
who needs blessing
the Unitarians rushing
knock knock who's
there   it is

no one

we're late   making
love in lovers'
galleys —
          proof "we" —

every broken, sometimes beautiful
immigrant—void O
                        da da da
similarity roiling

holding is a way of not
letting go he'd
said about paradox
but whatever was said
was said often
the opposite

no loss true

our bed is a made thing

like long strokes
attributing too much to impact
or apology
leaves one fallow

{ what he senses   when what he
   senses isn't my true—

          I rarely even go there }

one set of lips or
tongue beneath my age
& I concedes

conceit:

whatever
was said will be said
again   the opposition
equivocally true

they aren't what they are

chairs around a garden   fading
little pews   actually circum-plots
grave succinct things

stunning
how some second someone,
a *you* | I

never shows up
never showed up   never

caught "the train to the next…"
which is scripted, admittedly
oh-savior-like

but see how the luminous

seats   fading by luminous exploits
stained in yellow falling fruits
& bathed with earthly loam

exhume the sun

seeming as though thrones and horses

outlasting the body and later spaces 81 |

braying between the poles of time and less-ness,
always   it is contradictory   *on the one hand*
desire never a {dis}proof   like fulfillment

or *longing is natural*   appropriate too
where we locate it
Love   to be
in you   absolute too
in aestival tonguing

we are not space, fracas, nor lightly-go here

who being what is not space, fracas, nor lightly-go

here longs for what is inborn
what is absolute too   brays at the theremin of time
and less-ness always *it is contradiction*
on two hands   desire
never a {dis}proof or fulfillment

Love is in you   & aestival too
like longing dissolute
fulfillment our aestival proof

**I swear to you the beds here were born
with teeth**

        the great green speech of fallow

fragrant   our lawn halos   evening & alley
orangeness   almost dilatory   our back ways
our language certain   dilatory

                  beading with oak
trees   triangulations of—

glass   palings   & moon
sweat pea   tile   & thorn scent
the trivial turnway of alley, bike bell, & this

I swear to you

        we're born with teeth

there are expectation here   learn them
I am learning there are look-outs

anticipations

which are dilatory   weighted
like the seared eye unbolting
the fence in its tension of stake & climb
the sibling unable to age   mourn

there is a way of casting
this is stationary |

a want to write on the wall
a fear of not writing the right words on the wall
a tension in a hand
a tension with the man who with his hand
    painted the wall that wants to be wrote on

there is a fear of the writing on the wall
a love of triangulations which dilute me

my squirrel is a singer on the fence line
my watcher of the neighborhood foxtrot
my how fragrant the buds of the sweat peas he thieves

I am very messy with the long, long
not saying it in the kitchen make me the lightly-go one

& when I separate

maroon bells   anise hyssop   compact innocence
it's the tags not the roots that are shoddy

{Adventum}

ease & grace   god is
in us   & in us
all   all around us   god
chancing   the arrivals   god's/ours
o carriers   these in one
my singing god   so waitingly
hemming at blankets of water-
song   & my singing   o firebath

little wave of ease
& grace   love is
in us   & goodly
all   godly   around us
this chance of arrivals
his |hers
o caritas   four in one
my singing good Lovely
so gently
hewn by anchors & water
& fire   my singing   a fire
a timbre in the heart of thee

ease & grace You is
in me   & in me
complexly like anchors   blazes
arriving in watery scene
ships | hours   o certainly
ours is a singing
of chancery   say *equitas | embarazado*
invitations   hemmed on anchors
cry firebath of thee   cry
smolder me in grace

ease & grace   love is
in us   & in us
all   all roughly us   love
chanced   our arrivals
anchored hours
our little jars of heaven   granted
these in one hearth
o waitingly   done
my singing healer
this hymn for you
my blanket-fire-water-anchor
grace & ease to you
my song   & my singing
my god
              what will thee?

| *postlude* |

let it be said of us

&   fruits we left behind
that we too were viced   rotten
with poise & kingdom giveaways

let it be fleshy
the remembrance of our bodies
pear-shaped   swollen   halted

in the gateway arcing of neither
here-nor-there-thithery

plum polished on the silver table
pomme & anise & incensed

we gift strangely unexpected gifts
you wouldn't expect them

as slowly our hostess retracts

TEBOT BACH
A 501 (c) (3) Literary Arts Education Non Profit

THE TEBOT BACH MISSION: advancing literacy, strengthening community, and transforming life experiences with the power of poetry through readings, workshops, and publications.

THE TEBOT BACH PROGRAMS

1. A poetry reading and writing workshop series for venues such as homeless shelters, battered women's shelters, nursing homes, senior citizen daycare centers, Veterans organizations, hospitals, AIDS hospices, correctional facilities which serve under-represented populations. Participating poets include: John Balaban, Brendan Constantine, Megan Doherty, Richard Jones, Dorianne Laux, M.L. Leibler, Laurence Lieberman, Carol Moldaw, Patricia Smith, Arthur Sze, Carine Topal, Cecilia Woloch.

2. A poetry reading and writing workshop series for the community Southern California at large, and for schools K-University. The workshops feature local, national, and international teaching poets; Wanda Coleman, Amy Gerstler, Patricia Smith, Holly Prado, Dorothy Barresi, W.D. Ehrhart, Tom Lux, Rebecca Seiferle, Suzanne Lummis, Michael Datcher, B.H. Fairchild, Cecilia Woloch, Chris Abani, Laurel Ann Bogen, Sam Hamill, David Lehman, Christopher Buckley, Mark Doty.

3. A publishing component to give local, national, and international poets a venue for publishing and distribution.

Grateful acknowledgement is given to all of our supporters, the Tebot Bach board of directors, Steven R. and Lera B. Smith, and to Golden West College in Huntington Beach, California, all of whom make our programs possible.

Tebot Bach
Box 7887
Huntington Beach, CA 92615-7887
714-968-0905
www.tebotbach.org

This book is set in 9.5 point ITC Giovanni.